MEDIA SOURCES

COMPUTERS

Published by Creative Education
P.O. Box 227
Mankato, Minnesota 56002
Creative Education is an imprint of The Creative Company.

DESIGN AND PRODUCTION BY ZENO DESIGN

PHOTOGRAPHS BY Corbis (Bill Varie), Getty Images (Ian Cumming, Jan
Hakan Dahlstrom, Richard Du Toit, Michael Goldman, Gary Hunter,
Koichi Kamoshida, Raymond Kleboe, Raymond Kleboe/Stringer,
Lester Lefkowitz, Ron Levine, Gregor Schuster, Justin Sullivan, Chung
Sung-Jun/Staff, Nick Veasy, Vivid Images)

LIBRARY OF CONGRESS CATALOGING-IN-PUBLICATION DATA

Bodden, Valerie.
Computers / by Valerie Bodden.
p. cm. — (Media sources)
Includes index.
ISBN 978-1-58341-556-6
1. Computers—Juvenile literature. I. Title. II. Series.

QA76.23.B62 2008
004—dc22   2006101001

First edition

9 8 7 6 5 4 3 2 1

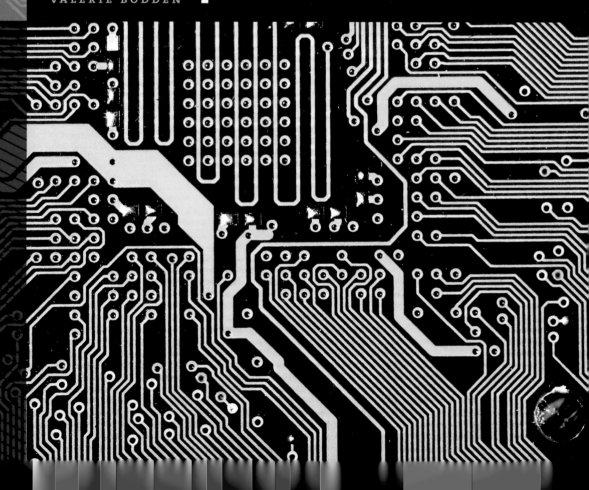

MEDIA SOURCES

Computers

VALERIE BODDEN

Computers are everywhere.
Most schools have computers.
So do most stores. You might
have a computer at home, too!

SOME OF THE FIRST COMPUTERS BROKE DOWN EVERY
SEVEN MINUTES! THEY HAD TO BE FIXED A LOT.

MANY KIDS USE COMPUTERS AT SCHOOL

The first computers were made about 70 years ago. They were very big. Some took up a whole room! But they could not do much. The computers had big tubes to make them work. The tubes broke a lot. Soon, new computers were made. They were smaller and did not use tubes. They used **chips**. Computers today still use chips.

EARLY COMPUTERS WERE BIG MACHINES

Computer chips are small. Some are as small as the point of a pencil! But they hold lots of information. They tell the computer what to do.

MANY THINGS HAVE COMPUTER CHIPS INSIDE OF THEM. PHONES AND CARS HAVE CHIPS IN THEM.

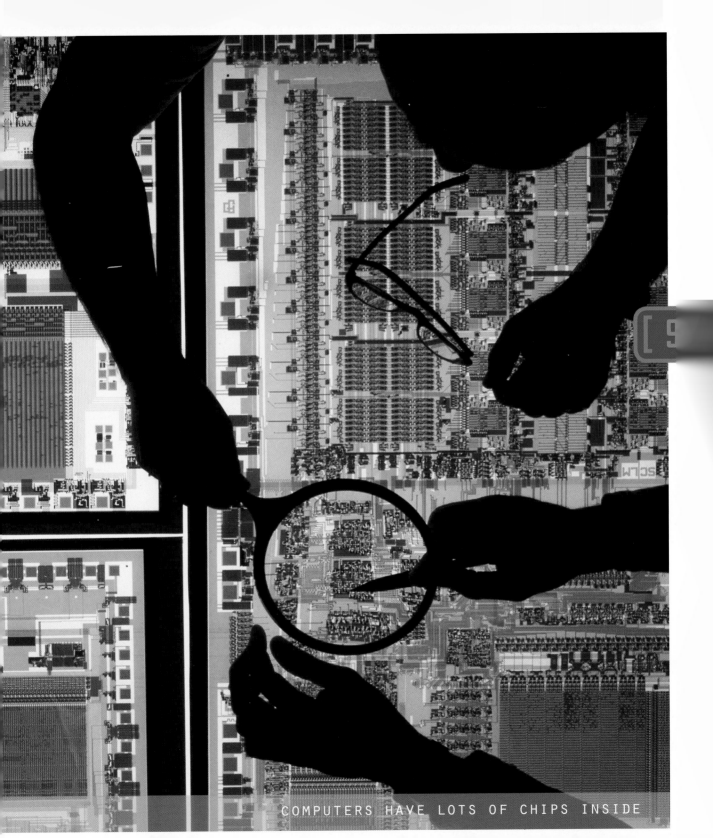

COMPUTERS HAVE LOTS OF CHIPS INSIDE

Today, there are all of kinds of computers. Some computers sit on desks. They are called "desktop" computers. Other computers are small. They can fit on your lap. They are called "laptops."

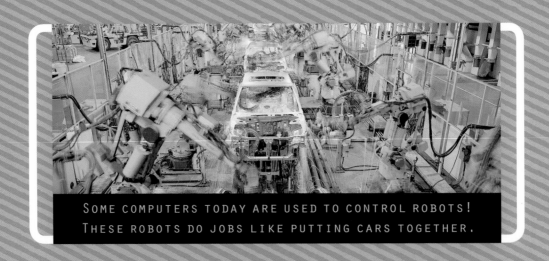

SOME COMPUTERS TODAY ARE USED TO CONTROL ROBOTS! THESE ROBOTS DO JOBS LIKE PUTTING CARS TOGETHER.

LAPTOP COMPUTERS CAN GO ANYWHERE

Some computers are huge. They are called "supercomputers." Supercomputers can do hard jobs. Some help people design airplanes. Others make maps of the weather.

MOST COMPUTERS LET YOU SAVE YOUR WORK. THAT WAY, WHEN THE COMPUTER IS TURNED OFF, YOUR WORK IS NOT LOST.

SUPERCOMPUTERS ARE BIG AND POWERFUL

All computers have lots of parts. The main part is the central processing unit. This is called the "CPU" for short. The CPU is where the computer does its work.

ONE OF THE FIRST COMPUTERS WEIGHED AS MUCH AS SIX ELEPHANTS PUT TOGETHER!

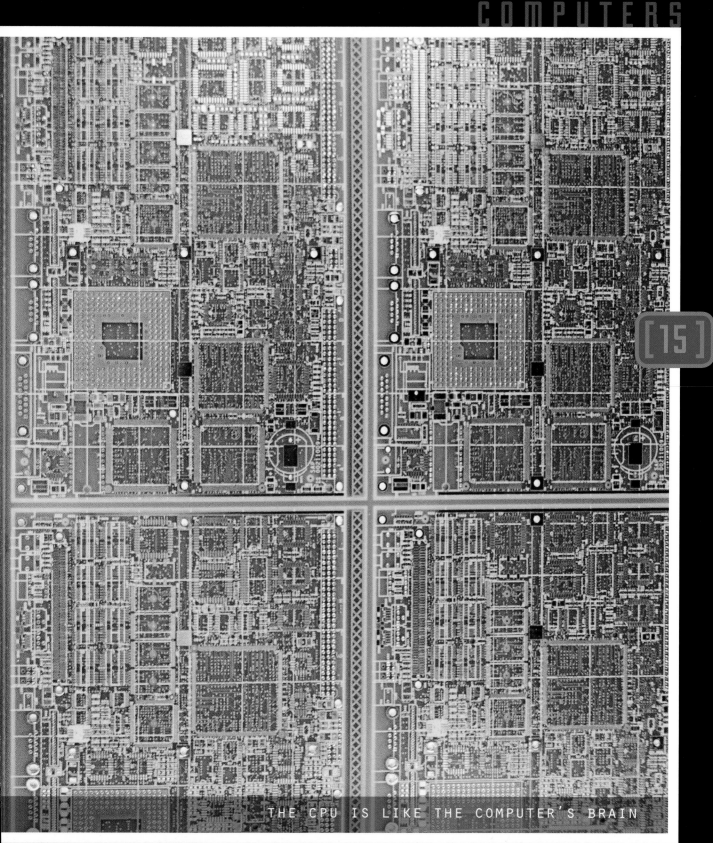

THE CPU IS LIKE THE COMPUTER'S BRAIN

Computers have screens, too. The screen lets you see what you are doing on the computer. Computers have a keyboard. You type on the keyboard. Most computers have a **mouse**. You slide the mouse to move a pointer on the screen.

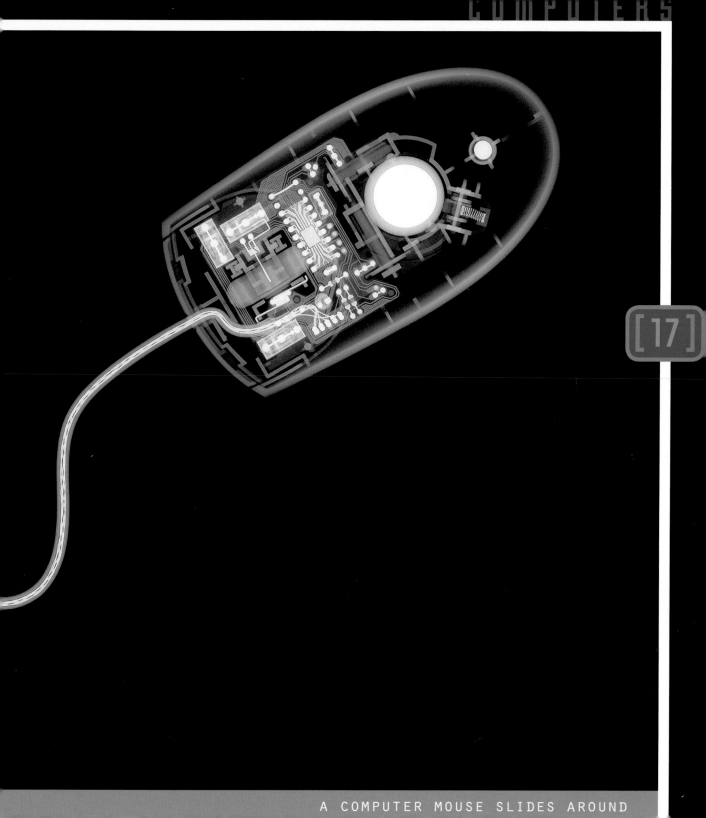

A COMPUTER MOUSE SLIDES AROUND

You can do lots of things with a computer. You can play games. You can type stories. You can go on the **Internet**.

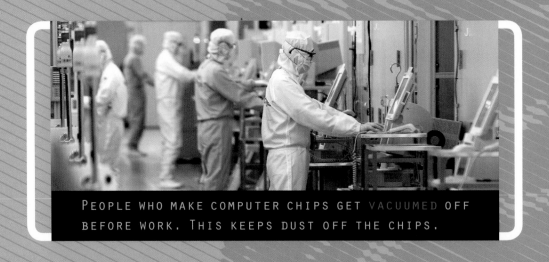

PEOPLE WHO MAKE COMPUTER CHIPS GET VACUUMED OFF BEFORE WORK. THIS KEEPS DUST OFF THE CHIPS.

STUDENTS CAN LEARN USING COMPUTERS

Today, **inventors** work to make better computers. They want to make computers smaller. They want to make them work faster. And they want to make them able to do more things. Then, people will use computers even more!

SOME COMPUTERS CAN HEAR PEOPLE TALK. THE COMPUTERS SHOW THEIR WORDS ON THE SCREEN!

NEW COMPUTERS HAVE COLORFUL SCREENS

GLOSSARY

chips very tiny computer parts; chips have lots of pieces on them that tell a computer how to run

Internet a system that joins together computers all around the world

inventors people who make new things that have never been made before

mouse a part of the computer that you slide to move the pointer across the screen

vacuumed cleaned off by a machine that sucks up dirt and dust

INDEX